Live Abroad
and
Keep Your
Career

THE GUIDE TO INTERNATIONAL
TELEWORKING

William J. Penhallegon

Live Abroad and Keep Your Career / William J. Penhallegon. —1st ed.

To Sybille – my everything.

Stuff your eyes with wonder, live as if you'd drop dead in ten seconds. See the world. It's more fantastic than any dream made or paid for in factories.

— Ray Bradbury

If you think adventure is dangerous, try routine; it is lethal.

— Paulo Coelho

AUTHOR'S NOTE

This book focuses primarily on the international teleworking component of living abroad, which means maintaining your U.S.-based, current career. In other words, your job, colleagues, customers, boss, etc. remain in the United States, while you reside elsewhere. This book is not about how to find a new job or start a new business in a foreign country, nor is it intended to be an exhaustive guide to the pure logistics of moving abroad and integrating into a local culture. The specifics for how to do that will vary widely by country and the web offers many helpful resources to answer your specific questions (including my website: www.teleworkabroad.com – more about that later). That being said, this book does include some of my bigger lessons learned in these areas when they might help inform your own thinking and planning.

In addition, the tax, social security, and other logistical considerations outlined in this book are specific to an American citizen employee working outside of the United States. However, the general questions to ask, the steps toward developing a proposal, the items to negotiate, and general teleworking strategies are applicable to almost anyone looking to move to a foreign country – regardless of where a job might be based.

Finally, I would like to note that this book is written from a general perspective and includes the experiences of other international teleworkers. Therefore, not all of the suggestions and implications necessarily apply to my personal situation and my agreement with my company.

Contents

Preface...1

Chapter 1: The Dream 5

   My Story 8

Chapter 2: Making the Decision 11

   Why Live Abroad 12

   Some Challenges of Living Abroad 14

   Living Abroad: Major Concerns that Probably Aren't...16

   Teleworking Abroad vs. Foreign Assignment 17

   Some Advantages of Teleworking Abroad....................19

   Some Challenges of Teleworking Abroad 21

   Selecting a Country..24

Chapter 3: Your Company's Perspective 29

   Permanent Establishment 30

   Social Security Tax Compliance 32

   Employee and Data Security.............................34

   Other Compliance Risks 35

   Management Supervision 36

   Benefits to Your Company 36

   Alternatives to International Telework 38

   You Don't Need to Have All the Answers Right Away...40

Chapter 4: Making Your Case **41**

    Step 1: Define Your Goals 42

    Step 2: Examine Your Current Work 43

    Step 3: Do Your Research 44

    Step 4: Audit Your Performance 47

    Step 5: Consider a Trial Run 48

    Step 6: Present Your Request 50

    Step 7: Negotiate... 53

    Step 8: Get It in Writing.. 57

Chapter 5: Making It Work **59**

    Your Workspace 60

    Work Discipline 61

    The Time Shift.. 62

    Staying In Touch 64

    Staying Engaged... 66

    Site Visits 68

    Checking In With Your Boss..................................... 74

    Other Resources 75

Chapter 6: Making the Move 77

    Moving Abroad 78

    Taxes 80

    Your Paycheck and Foreign Bank Accounts 83

    Certificate of Coverage 84

    Voting 85

    Health Insurance 85

    Estate Planning.. 86

    Investments 86

    More Help.. 87

Chapter 7: Making It Last 89

    Your Practical Limit.. 90

    Your Personal Limit.. 91

Chapter 8: In a Nutshell... 95

Postscript 101

Online Resources 103

Acknowledgements 105

Preface

The life you have led doesn't need to be the only life you have.

— Anna Quindlen

If you have ever *really* wanted to see more of the world, you may have dreamed about living in another country as a way to make it happen. But maybe you've not taken the idea any further because you are worried you might have to give up the security and benefits of your current career to do it. Well, good news! There is a way you can have the best of both worlds: become an international teleworker.

Just imagine. Work out of your home office during the day while being as close as you want to world-famous cities, historical sites, and stunning landscapes. Hop on the train to Paris one weekend; go skiing in the Swiss Alps the next – all without having to endure the hassle of long-distance travel. Or perhaps you are from another country, found a good job in the United States, and now want to return to where you grew up to be closer to your family. Whatever your interest, when you live abroad you may find your quality of life increase and your cost of living decrease. Best of all, you can do it while teleworking to maintain the security and financial stability of your current career path. The advantages to you and even your employer can be significant – so long as you know what you are getting into and avoid some of the potential traps along the way.

A few years ago, I decided to take the plunge and move abroad while maintaining my supervisory position with a U.S.-based firm. Other than starting a family, it's been the most rewarding endeavor of my life. Since then, I've had numerous people ask me: "How did you do it? How is it working out? What advice could you offer?" It turns out that there is surprisingly little "how to" information available to people interested in full-time teleworking, and even less for people interested in doing so from another country. It is therefore quite difficult for individuals and companies to know where to begin and what questions to start asking. This ended up being a major discovery process for me, with many lessons learned along the way. So I wrote this book to be the resource I wish I had when I was trying to figure it all out on my own.

If you find yourself wanting to change where you live but not what you do, this book will be your guide. Specifically, it will help you to:

1. *Decide if moving outside of the United States is something you really want to do.*

2. *Determine if doing your job remotely (i.e. teleworking) is feasible and a good fit for you.*

3. *Identify the questions you need to ask regarding taxes, social security, and other logistical implications of international teleworking.*

4. *Anticipate your management's perspective and the risks your company may be exposed to when you live abroad.*

5. *Develop your proposal for a telework agreement, and know what items you should be prepared to negotiate with your supervisor.*

6. *Implement your key strategies toward becoming a successful international teleworker.*

I will assume that since you are reading this book, you harbor some dream or ambition to live abroad. My intention is to give you the practical advice you need to accomplish this, while enabling you to maintain the comfort and security of staying in a job you currently enjoy. Being a remote supervisor and project lead gives me a unique dual perspective in that I understand telework and I understand what a manager will consider in allowing and extending an agreement. I've both requested telework for myself and I have considered telework proposals from people that work for me. Sitting on both sides of the table has provided me special insight into what each party is looking for, which I share in these pages to help you define realistic goals and negotiate your request with your management. Even if you are still only in the dream stage of this process, after reading this guide you will have a much better idea of what it takes to turn your vision into a reality.

CHAPTER 1

The Dream

Life begins at the end of your comfort zone.

— Neale Donald Walsch

For many people, living abroad feels like a dream. And no wonder! It's a big world out there. And sadly, most of us see so little of it. We work long hours and take little vacation time. And when we do use that precious time off, many of us conclude that it's easier to stay in the United States than to go abroad. When asked in surveys about what we would do if we had more time off, many Americans say international travel. However, U.S. State Department statistics show that as of 2017, only about 40% of Americans hold a passport – which suggests a disconnect in what we want and what we actually do.

Of course, America has a huge amount to offer workers and travelers, but at some point many of us start looking for more. We want to move outside our comfort zone to seek out new adventures, thrills, and challenges to overcome. Some of us want to learn a foreign language in a totally immersive environment. Some of us want to be within easy driving distance from ancient castles, world heritage sites, unique landscapes, and living history. Some of us have a spouse from another country, and we want to support them and get to know them better by spending some time living in their culture. Maybe some of us have young children and we'd like to bring them up in a different culture and educational system (and maybe even take advantage of practically free college). And maybe even some of us are from another country, found good jobs in the United States, and want to return to live where we grew up.

Whatever your reasons, it can be hard to satisfy them through a single two-week vacation per year (if we're lucky). But if you decide to LIVE abroad, the immersion is fully encompassing. Every weekend offers a new adventure. There's always more scenery, history, art, and culture around the corner, which can be explored deeply and at your leisure. No need to rush out of a world class art museum because you have to pack your bag and catch a plane! If you didn't see it all, just come back the next day. And if you or your spouse has family living abroad, you can spend more quality time with them and allow your children to get to know them better. Depending on your objective, the lifestyle and personal benefits of living overseas can be compelling.

Since you are reading this book, I probably don't have to convince you that it's important for us to get outside our cultural comfort zones. But the practicalities of doing so often seem daunting. It might be easy for natural entrepreneurs to set up shop in a foreign country, but many of us have spent time building up our current careers, enjoy what we do, like the people we work with, and are therefore reluctant to give it all up. All the same, we still find ourselves yearning for a lifestyle change. Wouldn't it be great to not have to sacrifice what we've worked for to do it? Can we truly move abroad while continuing to do the same work we enjoy?

The good news is that if your work allows you to telework stateside, you can probably adapt it to teleworking internationally. The independent workplace research and consulting firm GlobalWorkplaceAnalytics.com estimates that 50% of the U.S. workforce holds a job that is compatible with at least partial telework. You could be in that group if most of your work involves talking, reading, writing, coding, online research, etc. Modern communications are incredibly effective at bridging distances and allowing us to do this kind of work from anywhere we can find a reliable internet connection. And there are benefits to employers too. For example, GlobalWorkplaceAnalytics.com estimates that a typical business saves about $11,000 per teleworker per year.

So if you've ever dreamed about living abroad, there is a positive case to be made both for you and for your employer. This book will help you decide if international telework is a good fit for you, and then give you some insight into what you and your employer need to know to make it a reality. Of course, after giving full consideration to what it takes, you may find that international teleworking may not really be a good fit. And that's perfectly OK! But remember that you don't have to have all the answers figured out right away. You may not know for sure if or how it's going to work for you until you try.

My Story

Before we get started, I'll relate my personal story so you can see how I came to be such a believer in international telework. I grew up in Maryland and attended Virginia Tech, where I obtained undergraduate and graduate degrees in engineering. I entered the workforce in 1997, and since 2006 have been employed at a not-for-profit research and systems engineering company located in the Washington D.C. area. Much of what my work entails is probably typical for many people: reading and writing e-mails and reports, performing research and data analysis, and meeting with colleagues and customers. For a time my work required me to be on-site as I performed technical evaluations in my company's laboratory. However, as I describe later in this guide, I was eventually able to modify my job to give me the freedom to work from anywhere.

For years I hoarded every hour of vacation and worked my flex time to the maximum. This allowed me to take trips to Europe, Nepal, Pakistan, Antarctica, the Galapagos

Islands, South Africa, Vietnam, Indonesia, etc. But frankly, this wasn't enough. I'd been bitten hard by the travel bug and I wanted to see more of the world. I also wanted to immerse myself in a different lifestyle and take on the challenge of having to learn and get by in a foreign language.

My wife is originally from Germany and she spent 19 years living in the United States. We married in 2002 and have three children. But she was clear from the start that she intended to live again in Germany at some point, which suited me fine! I knew I wanted to scratch my travel itch by living abroad, but the question remained, how?

I fully admit I was lucky – I had been working for seven years for a company that treated me well, with great people, doing work I enjoy. To be honest, I felt like I'd won the job lottery and was therefore reluctant to let it go. So, I considered my options: go to work for a German company? Go into business for myself? Not go abroad after all, and ask my wife to sacrifice a dream that she and I both shared? After much reflection, I decided I didn't want to do any of these. I had worked hard to get to my current position, and I didn't like the idea of starting again at the bottom with a new company in a new industry. I'm also not an entrepreneur by nature, so the idea of starting my own business from scratch in a foreign land seemed risky, especially with a family to support. I was ultimately looking for something stable and long-term, from which I could continue building my career.

Eventually it dawned on me… why not just stay in my current job but do it remotely? Quite a few people in my company had teleworking agreements, though international telework was still quite rare. So, in 2013 I negotiated an agreement with my company and my wife and I moved our family to Germany. A few people in my company had tried teleworking abroad for short periods of time, but I was the first manager to pursue the option. Despite the risks involved for both me and the company, after some negotiation my management agreed to let me give it a try. I remember my boss telling me, "*You can do this, but it has to be transparent. It can't feel to me like you are on the other side of the ocean.*" It turns out that finding ways to ensure this transparency has been the key to my success as a long-term international teleworker. So now the group I supervise still works out of the Washington D.C. office, while I work from in Germany. My agreement can be terminated by my company if the arrangement becomes problematic, but so far it's working out better than I could have imagined!

Making this move and living abroad has been an amazing experience, full of adventures, challenges, and delights. The lifestyle here is far more suitable for raising my family than my wife and I found in Washington, and the *depth* of experience available to me as a resident of Germany is not something I could have found as a tourist. I am so grateful that international telework has enabled me to enjoy all this without having to sacrifice the work I enjoy. This has proven to be a successful journey for me, and now I want to help you figure out how to make it work for you!

CHAPTER 2

Making the Decision

You only live once, but if you do it right, once is enough.

— Mae West

Y ou can tell from my story that international tele-work was the right call for me. But will it be for you? There are three big questions you need to ask yourself as you contemplate your decision:

1. *Do I really want to live abroad?*

2. *Do I really want to telework – internationally?*

3. *Can I really make this work, given my current job and family circumstances?*

The fact that you are reading this book demonstrates that you have at least some interest in living life outside of the United States. In this chapter, I'll help you think it through by breaking down some of the advantages and challenges of being an American international teleworker. This is based on my own experience and from what I've learned in talking to other expats. Though I've tried to keep the discussion general, many considerations are specific by country and you should keep in mind that I'm writing this from the perspective of living in Western Europe.

Also note that immigration policy varies widely by country, and so the specifics of how to legally relocate to your target country are beyond the scope of this book. As you think about where you might want to move, you will need to research the requirements for obtaining a residence permit from your country of interest. I'll say a bit more about researching and selecting a country later in this chapter.

Why Live Abroad

It's easy to lose sight of the *vastness* of the United States until one experiences life in much smaller country. America certainly offers much to do and see; however, it can all be quite spread out – even in the cities. In contrast, smaller countries tend to be denser and one usually doesn't need to travel far to have a wide variety of experiences. From my home in Germany, for example, I can go skiing in the Black Forest one weekend, visit a thousand year-old castle on the Rhine the next, and then investigate some World War II historical sites the weekend after that. Such destinations being closer together, coupled with excellent public transportation, makes it easier to pack more living into a shorter amount of time.

Furthermore, when you live abroad you have greater flexibility in visiting sites that interest you – and discovering amazing new ones. Famous tourist destinations can get crowded during the busy seasons, which can significantly detract from the experience. But when you live closer to these famous sites, you can plan your visits for off-peak times and have a much more enjoyable stay.

Depending on where you live in the United States, you may also find yourself having a higher quality of life abroad. It's easy to fall prey to a grueling, grinding lifestyle in America, defined by an unhealthy work-life balance, whereas other societies place a higher emphasis on quality of life. I've found that even if you continue to work for an American company, it's easier to find your own personal balance when surrounded by people who work to live, as opposed to living to work. You don't feel the same pressure to work longer hours than necessary and maintain an appearance of being stressed out when you are surrounded by people who embrace relaxation and contentment. This is especially important if you have a family! Living abroad and working out of your home will likely give you significantly more quality time to spend with your loved ones – all with lots more to do and in closer proximity.

You may also find your cost of living to be lower than when you were in the United States. In some cases, salaries in other countries are lower than American salaries for equivalent occupations and levels of experience. As the local economy is based around these lower average salaries, you may find that you have greater purchasing power if you retain a salary based on the cost-of-living of a major American city – especially if the exchange rate between the dollar and your local currency works in your favor. And yes, tax rates can certainly be higher elsewhere than in the United States (especially in Europe), but depending on your situation you may be able to remain under the U.S. tax system. Even if not, the services and benefits of a more socialized system usually offset the higher tax rates. In Germany, for example, child care costs are subsidized by the government and can be drastically lower than in the United States. College is also subsidized, which could mean having to work fewer years before retirement! So for families with children especially, you may realize a significant financial advantage to living abroad, depending on the country you choose.

Some Challenges of Living Abroad

Of course, certain challenges come with living abroad as well. Leaving family and friends behind is probably the hardest. And depending on where you move, social integration can take a long time. Many cultures tend to be less transient than that of the United States, which means social circles have been in place since childhood. In some cases it may be difficult to join in – especially if you aren't yet fluent in the local language. On the other hand, many locals enjoy interacting with people from a different cultural background, and even practicing their English – which can be a terrific way to form friendships in your new country.

From my own personal experience, culture shock and homesickness are real. You don't always realize what you have and enjoy until they disappear. You will undoubtedly go through a period of missing certain amenities that come with life in America. (For me, since I now live in a small town, I miss restaurant and food variety. Unless you live in a major world city, it's hard to beat the sheer variety of restaurants and ingredients you find in America.) It doesn't take long, however, for expats to start focusing on what they've gained and find themselves missing their host country when they return to America.

Finally, there is the challenge of figuring out how life works – again. From house repairs to paying bills, from getting a cell phone plan to dealing with a fender bender... from taxes, insurance, and estate planning –almost everything needs to be relearned in accordance with local laws and customs. But this could also be looked at as part of the adventure! Indeed, you deepen your cultural integration the more you navigate these areas and interact with the locals. And you will gain an informed appreciation, for better or worse, about our equivalent systems in the United States.

Living Abroad: Major Concerns that Probably Aren't

There may be some matters that seem daunting or even prohibitive about living abroad, but in fact are probably more manageable than you think. One of these is staying in touch with friends and family. With Skype, Facebook, Instagram, etc. it's now easy to keep up with your loved ones back home. Plus, as you will likely be traveling back to your office on a semi-regular basis (see Site Visits in Chapter 5), you will have opportunities to catch up in person. Our modern tools for maintaining our connections work just as well from overseas as they do stateside; if anything you may find yourself more inclined to strengthen those relationships than when you are further away.

Also, don't worry about missing out on your favorite American TV, movies, radio, etc. Almost everything you'd ever want to watch is still easily available via the internet. But you'll want to immerse yourself anyway in the local media culture, and local programming offers an excellent way to do so.

Finally, you may have concerns about security and terrorism. Obviously, the risk varies by country, but in general most countries aren't any less safe on a personal level than the United States, and many are far safer. You quickly learn what areas to stay away from, just like in any American city or town. In all my travels, I've never encountered any hostility from anyone due to my nationality. Americans are still somewhat rare in many countries, especially outside of major cities, and so locals are usually curious and inquisitive when they meet one. Just be respectful, maintain your wits, and you will be fine.

Teleworking Abroad vs. Foreign Assignment

So, you've given it real consideration and want to try living abroad. And you'd rather not leave your company if possible. What are your options? First find out whether your company already has an international operation with American employees. If your skill set and interests are aligned with that group's core functions, your simplest path is probably to start applying for job openings in that group. There can be several advantages to getting assigned to an existing international operation. For example:

- These companies have formally worked out the implications for their employees working in those host countries, including taxes, social security, benefits, etc. Therefore the process and rules for living in that country are probably more straightforward than those involving a telework arrangement.
- The company will (probably) move you and pay you in the local currency (if desired).
- The company will (probably) help you with your international tax obligations and cover various expenses you will incur living abroad.
- You will be better able to keep normal hours since you'll mostly be interacting with people in your

own time zone. This increases your prospects for social integration both with your new department and the local culture (more on this below).

- This isn't really telework, after all. You will likely have an office outside your home requiring daily, face-to-face interaction with co-workers and customers – a pro for some employees and a con for others.

Sounds great – if it works out – but it may not be your best fit and there will be drawbacks regardless. Even if your company already has operations abroad, the work may be very different from what you currently do. Perhaps you want to stay within your technical area and continue interacting with your current colleagues, staff, and customers. As you consider this option, keep in mind the following potential disadvantages of transferring to your company's established international group:

- You may have to significantly refocus your occupational and technical specialty.
- You may have all new co-workers and customers. (Though for some people this could be a plus!)
- As these postings are sometimes treated by companies as a "perk," employees may be rotated in and out and your ability to remain in your position may be limited. Or, if the in-country work dries up or changes, you may find yourself no longer needed and forced to return home prematurely. Some peo-

ple may find it hard to adapt to this level of instability and uncertainty.

After considering the pros and cons, you may decide that it is best for you to stay in your current job while living abroad. In my case, I knew that I wanted to stay overseas for as long as possible, and reduce my risk of being pulled back due to forces beyond my control. So, I chose to create a path for myself as an international teleworker.

Some Advantages of Teleworking Abroad

Is teleworking, specifically *international* teleworking, a good fit for you? Think about it: much of the modern work day is spent going to meetings, talking on the phone, responding to e-mails, and writing reports. Why do that in a drab cubicle when it can easily be done from the comforts of your home office? And with modern communications, why does that home office need to be located in the United States? Depending on the nature of your job, you may be able to work pretty much anywhere in the world that offers a stable internet connection.

As you've probably discovered by now, there is surprisingly little information available to help guide someone considering full-time, international telework. So let us first consider some of the general advantages to you for full-time telework, whether stateside or international. These include:

- There is no need to maintain a work wardrobe, undertake a daily commute, or own a commuter vehicle. This saves you a great deal of personal time and money. In fact, GlobalWorkplaceAnalytics.com estimates that teleworking saves individuals anywhere from $2,000 to $7,000 per year. In my case, since I began teleworking, my family has downsized from three vehicles to one and saved thousands in the process.

- Your personal productivity may increase with fewer office distractions and no random drop-ins from colleagues. Plus, you can multitask while you are on the phone, listening in on meetings that require your attendance, but may have only a marginal relevance to your work.

- Your daily schedule will likely be more flexible, making it easier to achieve a better work/life balance.

- You may enjoy more quality time with your family. For example, you can share meals with them in the comfort of your home that you would normally spend in restaurants, the office break room, or at your desk.

The main advantages of working from a home abroad remain the same as being stateside. However, you may find at least two work-related advantages when working from a foreign country. First, depending on how many time zones away you are, you may enjoy several additional hours without any workplace distractions which can significantly increase your personal productivity (for more, see *The Time Shift* in Chapter 5). Second, if you have a career goal to increase your company's international presence, you will be in a better position to build the relationships necessary to accomplish it when you are closer to the people you are trying to reach.

In sum, the advantages to being abroad mostly relate to the personal benefits of experiencing new cultures and new ways of living. But teleworking, including from abroad, can enhance the *concentrative* aspects of your work by reducing or eliminating distractions and allowing you to prioritize your time and tasking. It can also, however, detract from the effectiveness of your *collaborative* work, as discussed next.

Some Challenges of Teleworking Abroad

Working remotely introduces its own set of challenges, mostly around how to collaborate effectively with others to get work done when face-to-face contact is significantly reduced. In my experience, the biggest difference when working far away from your colleagues is that it is much more costly, and thus much more difficult, to be in the office on short notice. As such, you need to realistically assess this challenge, plan your mitigations, and set expectations appropriately with the people you interact with. The major challenges of international telework are summarized in the list below, and more detail on many of these is included in subsequent chapters.

- Not all types of work are suited to being done remotely. You may need to adapt your current responsibilities to be able to perform your job from abroad (see *Examine Your Current Work* in Chapter 4).

- Some clients, customers, supervisors, and other stakeholders strongly prefer personal, face-to-face contact. Extra effort will likely be required on your part to reassure them that you are working diligently on their behalf and keeping up with your responsibilities.

- As with any teleworking arrangement, staying engaged with colleagues will require extra effort. Though sometimes a distraction, you will miss the random drop-ins from the people you work that sometimes lead to key insights or connections (see *Staying Engaged* in Chapter 5).

- Important meetings often require in-person attendance. When these are scheduled on short notice, you either have to incur the cost to attend or witness your job performance suffer in your absence.

- You may find that your work hours no longer have clearly defined start and stop times, and thus you end up working on and off throughout the day. This is exacerbated if you live in a different time zone, making it difficult to truly turn work "off" and focus on other aspects of your life.

- Working from a different time zone than your colleagues often leads to working odd hours (see *The Time Shift* in Chapter 5). This takes some getting used to, especially if you have a family. Also, the time shift may make it difficult to integrate into the local culture. For example, if you have the mornings off but work evenings to stay on the same schedule as your customers and colleagues, you may find it difficult to regularly engage in the social life of your new country.

- If one of your goals for moving abroad is to learn the local language, maintaining your English-speaking job reduces your opportunities for immersion.

- You may sacrifice upward mobility in the company as it may be difficult when working remotely to build and maintain the relationships necessary to make the move into management (see *Define Your Goals* in Chapter 4).

- And finally, recovering from job loss (or revocation of your telework agreement) may be difficult if you have established yourself internationally (for some possible mitigations, see *Your Personal Limit* in Chapter 7).

Teleworking abroad is clearly not be the best arrangement for everyone. But as you find yourself considering it, you may not know for sure if it's for you unless you give it a try. If this is the case, you might start working from home on a trial basis as suggested in Chapter 4 (see *Consider a Trial Run*).

Selecting a Country

Where you want to live is your own personal decision of course, and you will have to determine what appeals most to you in selecting your preferred location. Maybe you already have a host country in mind and you have a specific reason for why you want to live there. Or maybe you are just looking to gain an expat experience, even if you don't yet have a set destination. In either case, there are several important steps to take in assessing what it would be like to both live and work from your countries of interest.

First, if you aren't quite sure yet where you'd like to live, you can start your research by reading some travel books and thinking about the features you'd most like to have close-by. Big city or small town? Mountains or beach? Historical and cultural sites? Colorful nightlife? How near will you be to the things you most like to do? Reflect on any past vacations you've taken abroad and the travel experiences that left you feeling most energized. Where would you to return to and why? Also pay careful attention to guide book descriptions of the local cultures. Does a more traditional and conservative society appeal to you? Or would you rather live in a progressive and ever-changing community dynamic?

Keep in mind, however, that vacationing in a country can be a very different experience from actually moving and living there. So continue your research by exploring the practical implications of living in your country or countries of interest to avoid making a decision based purely on your emotional response to its culture and tourist sites. Whether you already have a region in mind, or are still narrowing down your selections, look at your targeted areas with the mindset of actually living there. Ask yourself: which region of that country would you want to move to and why? Would you want to live in a city or a small town? Does the local culture appeal to you enough such that you want to be immersed in it? Do you want to buy property or would you rent? If you have a family, are the schools acceptable? What is the cost of living and how is that affected by the current exchange rate? If you aren't yet fluent in the local language, how much of a challenge will that pose? Many countries have an official, or at least a dominant, religion. Will you have a difficult time if you do not subscribe to that faith? And, if you have a spouse and a family, what will they do? Are they as ready for the change as you are?

Our choice to live in Germany was clear from the start as my wife is from here and one of our goals was to live close to her family. I thought I knew Germany reasonably well from having visited several times before making the move. Our contacts and preparation helped us get the big stuff right, but still there were experiences related to living here that took me by surprise. These included a surprisingly strong community spirit, the high prioritization of a healthy work/life balance, and amazing investments in a family-oriented public infrastructure. But, coming from Washington D.C., I was also surprised at how noticeably homogeneous the culture is. America truly is an amazing melting pot and Germany is, well, mostly German. So before I arrived, I just didn't appreciate what it would be like integrating into a much more uniform society than I was otherwise used to. Though we were looking to have this deeper cultural experience, it still required a significant adaptation on my part and I recognize that it may not be for everyone.

Given this, you need a good sense of your targeted area's local lifestyle, amenities, practicalities, and hassles before you make your final decision. An excellent way to find these out is to travel to your top countries of interest and visit various non-tourist areas. What is the local housing like? Are the utilities reliable? Is the general infrastructure maintained or is it in a state of disrepair? Is the local government helpful or to be avoided? What are the more common types of local crimes? Also to help find answers, you could make contact with locals or expats through social media (such as a Facebook country expat group) and possibly meet up with them while you are visiting. They may even be willing to take you around and give you the inside story on your areas of interest.

As you research the pros and cons related to living in your country of choice, you will also need to consider what it will be like to work from home in that location as well. There are at least three critical requirements to look for as an aspiring international teleworker. First, you need a stable and reliable residential internet connection. Second, you need to be able to find a residence with sufficient room to set up an isolated, but comfortable, workspace (see *Your Workspace* in Chapter 5 for more). And third, you will need reasonable access to major transportation hubs to facilitate visits back to your work site. Carefully consider how difficult it would be for you to travel back to the United States when necessary, and so look at living in reasonable proximity to a train station or airport. Having these resources available will make your travel easier and more frequent, thus helping to ensure your long-term success.

Finally, in your country selection process, find out whether your company already has operations in your country or countries of interest. As described in Chapter 3, that might reduce some of the cost and administrative uncertainty for your company and make the difference in your request being accepted. And, as also described in Chapter 3 and Chapter 6, find out whether your country has tax treaty and Totalization Agreements with the United States. This will reduce your risk of double taxation on the same income.

There is obviously much to consider when selecting a country in which to live. But – don't let your research lead to paralysis. You will never really know what it's like to live somewhere until you try it. Your research goal should be to find out just enough to ensure a high probability of living the lifestyle you want, while satisfying the practical needs of teleworking internationally. And, you want to make sure you avoid, or at least be aware of, the risk of double taxation and any other major unexpected costs. Other than that, the surprises and discoveries along the way are what make this such an exciting journey!

CHAPTER 3

Your Company's Perspective

Ask yourself, is this good for the company?

— Bill Lumbergh, *Office Space* (1990)

I nternational teleworkers place burdens on companies that stateside teleworkers do not. For example, companies could be exposed to additional foreign income taxes, and they may incur significant legal costs to even find out their potential risk. They may also have to become aware of and comply with the laws of your host country to include physical worker safety, wage and hour laws, employee supervision, etc. As you develop your case, you will want to have some understanding of what risks your company will face in allowing you to do this, and be prepared to help mitigate them.

Obviously, the degree of risk will vary by country and your company will need professional advice to gain a full understanding of its exposure and costs. I am not a tax or legal expert and so the information in this chapter is not meant to constitute actionable advice. You and your company must consult professional international tax and risk experts to determine what will be required for your own personal situation. But if your management has no experience operating internationally, you can use the information here to help them identify the questions they will need to ask.

Permanent Establishment

First, you will want to find out as soon as possible whether your company already has operations in the country where you want to move. If so, it should already have a Permanent Establishment in that country and thus a good understanding of its costs and compliance risk. A Permanent Establishment is essentially a taxable business presence and involves a set of tests to determine whether the activities of your company are sufficient such that it will incur a tax liability in the host country. This can be a significant issue so if your company already has international operations, you may want to select your country from those in which it already does business. This way, there are likely to be fewer unknowns for you and for your management to deal with.

If your company has no international operations, or at least none in your country of choice, it may be at risk of triggering a new Permanent Establishment in that country and thus expose themselves to additional foreign corporate income taxes. An American teleworker working from home in a foreign country may not automatically trigger a Permanent Establishment, but there are specific criteria governed by tax treaties between the United States and your country of interest that increase the likelihood. The specifics vary, but in general your company will be at greater risk of establishing a Permanent Establishment, and thus incurring a tax risk, if:

1. *Your telework creates a "fixed place of business."*

2. *You are carrying out activities in that country that result in the generation of revenue.*

For example, if you are working out of your home office but only on projects or activities that generate revenue or create value solely for your company's U.S.-based operation, that may not be enough to trigger a Permanent Establishment. However, if while abroad you work on business development activities and generate local sales that benefit your company, you may have effectively set up a Permanent Establishment and your company could be faced with having to pay corporate income taxes to your host country.

The specifics vary by tax treaty and it may take some expensive legal work for your company to determine its risk. Unfortunately, even the cost of finding out whether this will be an issue could be a showstopper for your management. Before proceeding, you will want to research the Permanent Establishment triggers for your country of interest and have an idea for the types of work you plan to do and whether this will put your company at risk. (I've included some web links in the Resources section of my website that will get you started in researching and understanding the Permanent Establishment issue.).

Social Security Tax Compliance

Working abroad will also have certain social security implications for both you and your company, as most countries have some form of a social security tax that their citizens and residents are required to pay. Fortunately, however, the United States has Totalization agreements with many countries to help you avoid having to pay into each country's system simultaneously, against the same earnings. To take advantage of this, you must apply for a Certificate of Coverage (COC) via the U.S. Social Security Administration (SSA), which is the legal document you use to prove to your host country that you are already paying into the American system. You and your company's social security tax obligations will depend on the terms of the Totalization agreement between the United States and your host country, so you will want to be familiar with these as you develop your case.

As of 2018, the United States has Totalization agreements in place with the following countries: Australia, Austria, Belgium, Canada, Chile, the Czech Republic, Denmark, Finland, France, Germany, Greece, Hungary, Ireland, Italy, Japan, Luxembourg, the Netherlands, Norway, Poland, Portugal, the Slovak Republic, South Korea, Spain, Sweden, Switzerland, and the United Kingdom. Almost every agreement places a limit of five years for how long a U.S. worker can operate abroad under a COC. (Italy is the lone exception, which places no time limit on a COC.) If you plan to stay in your selected country for a period shorter than what your COC specifies, then you would continue to pay into the U.S. Social Security system – likely through your normal paycheck withholding. But if you plan to live in your host country past the COC duration, you will have to start paying into their system instead. Short extensions to the five-year time frames specified in the agreements are possible, and can be granted by the SSA without coordination with certain host countries. Longer extensions, however, need to be accepted by the host country on a case-by-case basis.

In the event that you plan to stay longer than what your COC specifies, your company may be exposed to compliance, reporting, and other costs for switching you over to the non-U.S. system. Your company may not be willing to assume this expense and so this is another area that you will need to understand regarding its potential cost exposure. Country-by-country Totalization Agreement detail and the COC application are available on the Social Security Administration website. (You can find direct links to the agreements and the COC application on the Resources area of my website and at the end of this book.)

Employee and Data Security

It is critical for modern companies to ensure the security of their employees, networks, and data. Thus you need to be aware of the additional security risks that come from being outside of the United States. This is especially important if you work on government projects and/or handle classified, sensitive, or propriety data. It's best to contact your corporate security office to understand the specific risks and concerns they may have, but this section reviews some points for you to consider.

First, your presence outside of the United States increases your foreign contact and makes you more removed from your company's security culture. You will be interacting daily with non-U.S. citizens and you may become a target of foreign intelligence gathering services or corporate espionage from foreign competitors to your company. Your company will likely need to provide you with special training to make sure you understand the risks and how to avoid them.

Second, if you work out of your home, your workspace will likely be less physically secure than your company's office in the United States. Does your work require you to hold sensitive or proprietary information on your laptop or personal computer? If your home is broken into and your computer is accessed or stolen, would that create a major data breach for your employer? Your company will have to evaluate its data security policy for your particular situation and may require you to encrypt your hard drive or even store your data only a network drive (instead of locally on your machine). Your company may require you to use a Virtual Private Network (VPN) or other security protocol to minimize the risk of your data being intercepted as you communicate with your colleagues. In extreme cases, your company may want you to harden access to your home office via extra door locks or window bars to prevent the likelihood of equipment theft.

In general, your company will need to ensure that they have appropriate security policies and technologies in place to protect you and your data in the event of an attack, and to maintain their network and broader data security should you become a target of a foreign interest.

Other Compliance Risks

Depending on where you chose to live, your company may be exposed to having to comply with local laws and ordnances in a variety of areas. For example, it may, as a matter of policy, monitor your computer use (internet use, e-mail, etc.), which may or may not conflict with privacy laws in other localities. There may also be local regulations with respect to home office ergonomics and safety that your company would need to be in compliance with. In addition, your company would need to understand if the government of your selected country considers you covered under its local wage and time off regulations. And if so, whether they would face a penalty for you not adhering to them.

Management Supervision

Perhaps your company already has a robust telework policy and experience supervising employees that are not regularly on site. If so, it may not be difficult to adapt and apply these policies to someone living abroad. However, if your company is new to allowing employees to telework, it will need to establish management and supervisory procedures to ensure your happiness and productivity as a worker. You can help by developing and communicating your own strategy to remain engaged with your boss, colleagues, and customers. (See Chapter 5 for a discussion of successful teleworking practices.)

Benefits to Your Company

So far this chapter has focused on the potential risks, costs, and other challenges to allowing you to telework internationally. This is important as you and your employer need to enter into this agreement with as realistic an assessment as possible to ensure long-term success. However, there are potential upsides for your employer as well.

First, depending on how strongly your intent is to live abroad, your company will maintain you as an employee. Is your desire to be abroad strong enough such that you might leave your firm and join a competitor? Finding and training good workers is time-consuming and expensive, and it may be worth it to your boss to allow you to do this to keep you on staff. Your retention is especially important if you bring new work into your group. But before counting on this, honestly assess your value to your company. (See Perform a Self-Evaluation in Chapter 4 for more about this.)

Second, your company will consider the benefits of not having to provide you with physical office space. This may decrease their utility cost, rent or required office space, and also eliminate the need for any transit subsides they may otherwise provide. As noted earlier, the independent workplace research and consulting firm GlobalWorkplaceAnalytics.com estimates that allowing an individual to telework saves a typical business up to $11,000 per year. In addition, the U.S. Office of Personnel Management provided a report to Congress in November 2017 summarizing the status of telework across the Federal Government. The report describes various expected benefits and challenges to the government in encouraging telework; its findings may be helpful to you in preparing your case to your management. (A link to the report is available in the Resources section of my website.)

Finally, your employer will likely consider the specific benefits of you being abroad. For example, this move could put you in a position to build new business opportunities and relationships overseas. (Be careful, though, about triggering a Permanent Establishment.) Can your company use your story in its marketing and recruiting campaigns, to bolster its global image and demonstrate how well it accommodates its employees? Are there local compliance laws in your country of interest that are less stringent than those of the United States, which might reduce your company's costs? As you can see, it's important to consider what might constitute a positive business case for your management in addition to the potential risks.

Alternatives to International Telework

If it appears that your international telework may trigger a Permanent Establishment, social security, and/or other compliance costs, any of which might result in your company denying your request, there are alternatives that you can consider to still live abroad and keep your career.

Global Employment Outsourcing

One workaround may be for you to use a third-party, global employment outsourcing service. This refers to transferring your employment to a company that is legally established in your country of interest, but then being hired back out to your original company as a contractor. These companies are usually referred to as International Professional Employer Organizations (PEOs) and they handle the administrative, legal, tax compliance, and related burdens that your company would otherwise face in setting up a business entity in your country of interest.

The PEO becomes your official employer, which obviously severs your current employment relationship. Be aware that this has implications for your benefits package and matching retirement contributions, but if you pursue this path, these items may be negotiable as part of the contract. But this is a way you can continue on your current career path, while helping your country avoid new tax risks and compliance costs. These PEO companies typically levy a fee on your employer to put you on contract, but this may be offset through reduced cost exposure and benefits obligations. If your company has no experience in this area, you might want to do some of the research to help them understand and mitigate their risk via these third-party employment services. (See the Resources section on my website for links to more information about Global Employment Outsourcing and PEOs, including some companies that offer this service.)

Independent Contractor

Another possibility is to resign and become an independent contractor or consultant back to your original company. Once you relocate to your country of interest, you will be responsible for complying with local regulations and tax filings as a "self-employed" person. This will eliminate the international regulatory compliance costs and risks to your employer, but the downside is that the burden now falls on you to find out the requirements for operating in your country of interest. This is not the easiest path, but it still may be worth exploring if the permanent establishment issue proves to be insurmountable for your company.

You Don't Need to Have All the Answers Right Away

It is beyond the scope of this book to detail all of the factors your company will need to consider when allowing you to work from abroad. This section was not intended to provide a complete list of concerns that your company may have, but it should cover most of the significant issues. Accountingweb.com has put together a "Checklist for International Telecommuting" that covers many of the questions your company will need to have answered as they consider retaining employees abroad. You may find it useful to review as well, to ensure you understand any potential showstoppers and to strengthen your proposal and negotiating position. (A link to the checklist is provided in the Resources section of this book and on my website.)

Researching the full scope of these issues may seem daunting. And rightly so – international agreements tend to be complicated. But you don't need to have all the answers figured out ahead of time in order to proceed with your management. If they are open to the arrangement after hearing your case, they will consult with their attorneys and tax experts to determine the next steps. But at each point in the process, the more you understand the potential obligations your company will face, the better prepared you will be to respond to your management's concerns or objections.

CHAPTER 4

Making Your Case

If opportunity doesn't knock, build a door.

— Milton Berle

So now you have decided that you want to live abroad and have selected a country. Maybe you've even found a fit there with one of your company's international operations. Terrific! Start contacting the managers of those departments and applying for openings, as you would with any other internal transfer. But if you decide (like I did) that you want to stay in your current job, how do you go about making the case to your company? You need to continue your research and develop a plan. This chapter describes at least one path forward from here.

Step 1: Define Your Goals

First, think about what you really want and write it down. Ask yourself: what do you hope to get out of living abroad, and how long do you want to be away? Do you have a fixed timeframe in mind or do you want to just see what happens? Is it compatible with your career goals? For example, do you want to advance technically in your current job or climb the management ladder in your company? While the former is a realistic goal for teleworkers, the latter may not be, as it can be challenging to move up in management without being on-site to develop or maintain the necessary relationships. However, if your goal is to enhance your company's international presence, living abroad may be an effective way to pursue it.

Also consider the importance of this move to you personally, and what you are willing to sacrifice to make it happen. For example, can you afford to take trips back to your work site if your company won't cover the cost? Are you comfortable shifting the majority of your interactions with your customers and colleagues to the telephone? Are you willing to possibly slow your ascent up the corporate ladder, if necessary?

And, how amenable will this move be for your family? Is it compatible with their goals? Will your spouse make sacrifices to live abroad as well? Are you comfortable putting your kids in a foreign school system? If it's inferior to the education they would receive in the United States, do you think you can you fill the gap?

In essence, before you start putting all of this in motion, you need to have an honest conversation with yourself and your family about why you want to do this, how long you want to be away, how compatible it is with your career goals, what you are willing to sacrifice to make it happen, and what to do if it doesn't work out the way you planned.

Step 2: Examine Your Current Work

You need to determine early on if the nature of your current job is compatible with working remotely. If most of your work involves talking, reading, writing, coding, online research, etc. – there's probably little that ties your job to a specific place. Modern communications are incredibly effective of bridging the distance. Losing face-to-face contact can be a challenge, especially when trying to build new relationships, but it can be overcome.

The situation may be more difficult if your job is, say, tied to a laboratory with specialized equipment located at your work site. If so, you need to consider the importance of that tie and what you can do to reduce it. If you don't need continuous access, can you negotiate an agreement to return to your work site on an as-needed basis? Can you build a team or network that remains on site to handle those aspects of the work for you? Bear in mind, you may need to change your job within the company, or at least the nature of your current work, before you can consider moving abroad.

This was a major barrier for me at one point. In the first part of my career, I was in my company's laboratory leading engineering evaluations that required specific facilities. I had to be in our lab on an almost a daily basis, thus doing my job remotely would not have been possible. However, I was eventually promoted to be a project leader and my responsibilities now include supervising engineers who conduct the evaluations, instead of leading them myself. This still requires extensive communication, but I no longer need to be in the lab as often. I can't completely sever my ties with my company's technical facilities, however, and so I still return three to four times per year and plan my trips around natural milestones to check in on my team's progress. In my case, a job change allowed me to start working remotely while staying in the same field and continuing to work with my colleagues.

Step 3: Do Your Research

Obviously, research and preparation are important before presenting your proposal to management. You need to understand the attitude of your boss (and company) toward teleworking in general and the challenges they will face in enabling you to do it internationally. Will you need to sell them on teleworking in general, or only on the international aspect? Does your company already have several international teleworkers, or will you be a trailblazer? How might this arrangement benefit your organization? You need to anticipate the potential concerns and issues your company will face in order to tailor your proposal and convince your management that you've thought this through.

First, find out if there is anyone in your company who is already teleworking, especially internationally. If so, seek them out to learn how their experience went. They will offer invaluable guidance on the specifics of negotiating potential challenges and objections. Take many notes. (My company has few international teleworkers and thus I am often approached by colleagues asking me how I did it. As I noted in the Preface, this is what gave me the idea to write this book!)

Existing Policy

Does your company already have a teleworking policy in place, either stateside or international? If not, you probably have some groundwork to do with your human resources department to help create one. (Establishing this from scratch would be a unique process to each company and is thus beyond the scope of this book. However, the Resources section of my website includes a link to sample policies and agreements.) If your company only has a domestic telework policy, still ask human resources for a copy. Can it be easily adapted for international work? Is it compatible with your vision of how you want to work? Or are there any restrictions that may be prohibitive? What aspects of it are negotiable?

Employer Benefits

As described in Chapter 3, you will want to research the potential benefits that teleworking will have for your employer. For example, will they save money by not having to provide you with physical office space? Will this put you in a position to build new business opportunities and relationships overseas? Will it enhance your company's international presence or make it more attractive to potential recruits? Be sure to have done some initial research into the potential benefits so you can put together a positive business case for your management.

Your Company's Risks

You will want to understand the income tax and social security risk your company will potentially be exposed to, as described in Chapter 3. Again, this does not mean that you need to come up with all the answers ahead of time, but you will at least want to be able to show that you've done your homework and understand what you're asking of them. If you suspect that triggering a Permanent Establishment may be a deal breaker for your company in agreeing to let you keep your job while you live abroad, you may want to research and even contact International PEOs to see how they could help your company avoid its exposure to new costs.

Step 4: Audit Your Performance

So, you think the nature of your work lends itself to working remotely and your research has not uncovered any showstoppers. When is the right time to approach your boss? A key point to consider well before making the request is how valuable you've been to your organization. This requires some honest career and performance reflection. Do you typically get above average performance reviews? Are there problem areas that need to be addressed first?

The truth is that allowing you to telework, especially internationally, would require your company to place significant trust in you. It also places an extra burden on your management to tackle the logistics and other complications it will bring. Even if you are doing a great job for your company, you need to consider how to make yourself as *irreplaceable* as possible, beyond simply doing good work.

It's obviously a good idea to do this anyway, but you need to be regarded by your management as an invaluable employee – one who would be extremely hard to replace. Your boss will be faced with a decision about whether it's better for her to retain you and keep you happy, or if it's easier to replace you with someone willing to work out of the office. You need to go into the negotiation from a position of strength, by realistically appraising what you bring to your job. Ask yourself: if you were in your boss's position, would you say yes? Would you be willing to put up with the potential hassle of managing you remotely, or would you feel inclined to look for someone else who can do your job instead?

If your answers to these questions give you pause, you may need to do some career development before approaching your boss. This could involve a couple of years working extra hard to better establish yourself and bolster your position. Develop strong relationships throughout your management chain and make sure that your work is both visible and irreplaceable. Do you have key relationships with customers, and are you regularly bringing in new work that would dry up if you left? When you walk into your boss's office to make your case, you should feel confident that she knows she can't afford to lose you.

Step 5: Consider a Trial Run

Full-time teleworking may not be the best fit for everyone – and perhaps you still aren't sure if it's for you. One way to find out is through a trial run, perhaps by working from home a few days a week at the start, building up to full-time. Once that starts feeling natural, you can then consider making the leap.

The steps to setting up a trial run would be the same as with a traditional, stateside work-from-home telework agreement. The main difference is that you know you are close to the office and can be there on short notice in person, whenever something important pops up. When you telework internationally, this will no longer be possible. So as you perform a trial run, it's important to keep in mind that the flexibility you enjoy when working close to your site will not be there once you move.

Still, a trial run will provide valuable insights into your potential for remote telework. You will gain a sense for how collaborative your job truly is, and the challenges you will face in trying to maintain that from off-site. You will also be forced to learn about the various communication technologies you can use to stay in touch with your colleagues. Once you are adept at using them from your current home, they will work the same way when you are abroad. And, your colleagues will get used to interacting with you via technology instead of face-to-face. This will help ensure that the difference for them won't be as stark once you are finally abroad.

A trial run will also help you learn about how much more productive you can be with concentrative work, when your day-to-day distractions are reduced. You may even find that as your productivity increases, your value as an employee increases! This would prove to your management that you can make this type of arrangement work, which should lead them to be more willing to accept the hassle and cost on their end for you to live abroad.

Finally, and most importantly, you will learn if working out of your home is right for you before you commit to a major move. Some people thrive on regular face-to-face contact and would rather not be at home for most of the day. Others find it too difficult to avoid home-based distractions while they are trying to work. If you have these concerns, a trial run will help you determine their serious-ness ahead of time.

When requesting a trial run, you may or may not want to let your management know up front that your ultimate intention is to move abroad. Depending on your relation-ship with your boss, the right time to ask may not be until after you've proven capable of sustaining remote employ-ment. But no matter what, be honest! If, for example, you have a foreign spouse and you want to live abroad to get to know him or her better, your management may suspect that your request to work from home is a trial run for a more significant change. So, if asked, you will want to be honest that you are considering this option, and explain your rea-sons why.

Step 6: Present Your Request

Ok – you think you can adapt your job to working re-motely, you've done your homework, you are valuable to your company, and you are ready to make your proposal. Now you need to decide the best format to obtain a favora-ble response from your boss. Should you bring it up during a friendly conversation in her office? Or would she be more receptive to a formal proposal, even one involving slides? Do you want to schedule a meeting with her and provide some advance notice of the topic? Whatever format you choose, you want to prove to her that you've thought this through. Therefore your request should include at least some of the following:

- Start with the basics. Describe your intent to live abroad. Where do you want to move to and why? When are you looking to make the move and how long do you want to stay?
- Explain why it won't negatively affect your work. For example: "Most of my day is spent on the phone and in front of the computer. I can do that as easily from another location as I can from here."
- Related to the last point, emphasize how you intend to make this as transparent as possible. What you will want to show is that you have a strategy to stay on top of the work and in touch with your customers and colleagues (see *Staying Engaged* in Chapter 5).
- If you have experience leading or being part of remote or virtual teams, especially with members that span various time zones, emphasize that you've already demonstrated your ability to thrive in this type of situation. Explain how this arrangement will not be a major departure from the way you work currently.
- Share any direct benefits to the company that you found in the course of your research. For example, you might suggest the cost savings for you to work from home, or the potential opportunity to expand the business to new markets (though in this example, be ready to discuss the risk of this triggering a Permanent Establishment).

- Describe how this could improve your work productivity. For example, when you work in a different time zone, you'll have some hours where you can focus without distraction from e-mails and drop-ins (see *The Time Shift* in Chapter 5). But be careful here, as you don't want to give the impression that your current productivity isn't all it could be.

- If your company already has a robust teleworker policy, you can discuss how this arrangement would function in much the same way.

- If your job involves working with sensitive or proprietary data, you may want to be prepared to talk about your personal and data security strategy.

If you suspect that triggering a Permanent Establishment and other issues discussed in Chapter 3 are likely to be major issues, you can still structure your proposal in much the same way to get the initial buy-in from your management. Then you can proceed to work with your company to assess the actual risk they face and whether you need to consider continuing your work via a PEO or as an independent consultant. If you take this approach, you will need to work with your management and your human resources and legal departments to determine the implications and risk of severing your direct employment with your organization.

It's important for your boss to buy in to the benefits of your teleworking arrangement as she will be your advocate as your request moves up the management chain for final approval. You need to demonstrate that you've carefully considered this arrangement both from your perspective and hers. The bottom line is that if your company can ill afford to lose you and your boss knows it, you will likely find management approvals more forthcoming.

Step 7: Negotiate

The initial proposal goes well and your management has agreed to work with you on crafting an agreement. Now it's time to negotiate terms! As with any negotiation, anticipate what is in the interest of the other party and then have a strategy to provide it in a mutually beneficial way. In general, your management will be looking for the following:

1. *You will maintain your productivity and work quality?*

2. *Minimal to no additional costs or burdensome oversight required?*

3. *Any likely benefits for the company?*

You will likely have already covered these in your proposal to the best of your ability. However, management may inform you of other issues that you didn't consider. Since your best chance of putting a successful agreement in place is to minimize the cost and hassle to your employer, you'll want to hear their concerns and adapt your proposal and strategy to mitigate them. As you enter the negotiation process, know in advance what you are willing or unwilling to accept in exchange for this opportunity. In other words, consider your requirements beforehand and be ready to negotiate at least some of the following areas:

Departure Date

When do you want to leave? How much time do you need to get your personal affairs in order, wrap up any projects requiring your in-person attention, and to prepare your customers and colleagues for your departure? Discuss with your management how long they will need to research the company's obligations and process the transition.

I recommend giving yourself at least six months to plan and execute your transition, though a year is probably better. When you arrive in your country, you will also want to ensure you have enough vacation time to get yourself established before you need to begin work. So if necessary, consider delaying your departure date to maximize your available time off for when you arrive.

Duration

What are the terms for the length of time you will be away? Will you have to come back after a set amount of time, or is your company willing to let you stay indefinitely, so long as it's working out? What will each side look for in determining whether or not it is working out? How much notice will your company give you if it decides to cancel your agreement?

Also, do you plan to stay past the duration specified in your Certificate of Coverage? (See *Social Security Tax Compliance* in Chapter 3.) If so, is your company willing to assume any additional compliance and reporting costs? Would you be willing to bear those costs yourself?

Work Hours

What schedule are you going to keep? How much will your work hours overlap with your company's core hours? (See *The Time Shift* in Chapter 5.) What will be your availability? If meetings are scheduled for times outside of your main work hours, will you be flexible enough to still attend them?

Site Visits

How often will you return to your main work site? Unless you truly do work in a vacuum with minimal interactions with your customers and colleagues, plan to make occasional trips back to the office. People will start forgetting about you if they don't see your face very often, even if you are regularly on the phone. How often will depend on your situation, but I personally find it worthwhile to travel back to the office three to four times a year, for a couple weeks at a time.

Given the need for return visits, who will pay for your travel? These trips constitute a significant expense and perhaps your worth to the company is such that it is willing to assume it for you. But, perhaps not. If you don't expect your management to be willing to pay for your travel, you might find out whether it pays for travel for domestic tele-workers. You could estimate a sum for what stateside tele-working travel would cost, ask your company to cover up to that point, and then offer to pay that the difference.

If you are worried that your negotiating position is weak, you may consider offering to pay some or even all of your expenses related to your site visits, at least initially. For example, you might pay for your flights and then ask your company to pay for your rental car and hotel while you are in town. If this ends up being the case, there are numerous strategies you can use to reduce your costs, such as paying for planes tickets during the off-seasons and us-ing frequent flier miles during peak seasons when the costs are highest. If your willingness to assume the travel costs for this is what it takes to get an agreement in place, you could start paying out-of-pocket and then renegotiate more cost sharing with your management later, once they see it's working out and that you are saving them money overall. See *Site Visits* in Chapter 5 for more about when to sched-ule site visits, how to make them effective, and some strat-egies to reduce your personal travel costs.

Telecommunications Equipment

What equipment will your company provide to help keep you in the loop? Will they give you specialized gear, such as a headset or VoIP phone? Or will you be expected to make do with, say, only your laptop and a headset? Will they provide you with a company cell phone or will you need to procure your own once you've moved? (See *Stay-*

ing in Touch in Chapter 5 for more about equipment considerations.) And, if you terminate your employment with them but remain abroad, how will company equipment be returned? Will you be obligated to pay for shipping it back?

Logistics Expenses

How much will your company be willing to help you move and get acclimated to your new country? Again, this may depend on how much they value you as an employee. In the best case, perhaps you can negotiate for them to pay for your move and other expenses. Or, maybe they will allow you to use the services they provide to their non-telework international employees, such as access to an international health insurance policy and income tax preparation.

Finally, think about how "hard-nosed" you want to be in these negotiations. Your chance of success will be greater if you show some good faith toward your company and are willing to assume some expenses on your own. After all, you are asking for this opportunity and for them to assume some level of burden on their end; thus it is not unreasonable for you to do the same.

Step 8: Get It in Writing

Once you and your management have negotiated the terms, they should be codified via a formal teleworking agreement. This protects you and your company from any misaligned expectations. Most companies already have telework agreement policies, but if yours doesn't work with your management and human resources department to draft one that covers the various points of negotiation. GlobalWork-placeAnalystics.com provides some sample policies and agreements that you can use as a foundation. (See the Resources section of my website for a link.)

CHAPTER 5

Making It Work

*The most difficult thing is the decision to act, the
rest is merely tenacity. The fears are paper
tigers. You can do anything you decide to do.*

— Amelia Earhart

You have an agreement in place and are getting
ready to go. Congratulations! Now how do you
make sure you are successful? Like stateside
telework, you will need a distraction-free workspace in
your home and the discipline to stay focused during your
work hours. This chapter will cover some of that, but focuses more on the unique aspects of fulfilling an international teleworking arrangement.

Your Workspace

Your physical workspace requirements are largely the same as with stateside teleworking. You will want a dedicated home office that is isolated from daily distractions and noise elsewhere in your residence. This is especially important if you have a family, as you won't want to allow the commotion of the kids coming home from school and their playtimes to interfere with your concentration and phone communications. Your home office should be a comfortable space for you, as you will spend many hours a day at your desk and you want to make sure you do not dread being there. However, while making your space comfortable, be sure to not go overboard in filling it with distracting personal effects and toys. You do need to make sure your workspace has sufficient space for books, papers, files, etc. so that what you need to do your job is readily accessible and you remain organized. Working from your kitchen table may be sufficient for a part-time arrangement, but it's critical to have a dedicated, isolated, comfortable workspace when you telework full-time.

Depending on the nature of your work, you may also need to consider your physical and data security – especially since you are no longer in the United States. As described in Chapter 3, your company may require you to take extra precautions if you handle sensitive or proprietary data. As you research your company's security policies, you will want to consider whether any modifications to your home workspace will be required to ensure compliance. For example, you may need to harden access to your home office via extra door locks or window bars to prevent an intruder from stealing your computer or other equipment. In another example, your company may not consider a Wi-Fi connection to be sufficiently secure. Therefore you may be required to directly connect computer and router with a cable, which could be a challenge depending on your home configuration. Be sure to schedule a discussion with your company's security department if you have any concerns about how to ensure the integrity of your workspace.

Work Discipline

As you work from home and out of the direct line-of-sight of your supervisor, you must ensure your personal discipline stays high in remaining focused and on task. Distractions are everywhere and can be quite difficult to avoid. So begin by establishing a clear separation between your home life and your work time, and set expectations with your family for minimizing interruptions while you are on the job. Make sure your spouse and children know your core work hours and are clear about when they can approach you. And keep the most distracting toys out of your workspace! It can be tempting to squeeze in a video game between work calls, so make it easier on yourself by keeping the console elsewhere in the house. It is true that pauses and distractions sometimes help your mind work through difficult problems subconsciously, which can lead to breakthroughs. These are exceptional cases, however. Take a walk if you need a short break and strive to be as focused, disciplined, and productive at home as you would be if your boss was right next door.

Good time management skills are a must and you will need to develop a system that works for you to remain disciplined with your work. I personally live my life by my calendar and my "To Do" list. I block off times on my schedule to focus on specific tasks and I keep lists of what I need to accomplish daily and weekly. I then make sure to check these things off before I allow myself to become distracted by the family and other endeavors. So whatever system you use now to stay organized, you must ensure its effectiveness once you are no longer surrounded by colleagues and customers that help you stay on task. Be open to finding new ways of working if you find it difficult to keep your focus under your current method.

The Time Shift

Maybe you are only moving north or south and will remain on a time zone close to your work site. If so, that will make the adjustment easier. But for employees moving overseas, managing your workload to comport with the core hours of your colleagues and customers will require a major shift in your schedule. As noted earlier, your odds of success increase the more transparent your remoteness is to your management. The key is *availability*. Remember, as much as possible, you don't want people to notice that you are an ocean away or in a different time zone. When your customers, boss, and colleagues need you, you're there.

This means that at least some of your work hours should overlap with the core hours of your co-workers. How much though is a matter of negotiation. If you wind up moving east of your work site, for example, your day will start sooner than that of your colleagues. You might find yourself taking the mornings off, starting work around lunchtime, and then working into the night. Obviously, you need to consider what impact this will have on your family. In this case, working from home may allow you to have meals with your spouse and children, but you may not be available for other evening activities. Or in another example, you might negotiate to keep core work site hours Monday through Thursday, but then only work your local morning / afternoon hours on Fridays.

In Germany I'm six hours ahead of my work site in Washington D.C. I am fortunate to have flex time, which means that I keep core hours but have some latitude to distribute my time within a reporting period as the work itself demands. I've had success keeping regular work hours that match up with East Coast morning hours. On days where there are few or no scheduled afternoon calls or meetings, I work my local mornings and don't work into the night. However, ad hoc and pop-up meetings are common occurrences. So sometimes even after working a full local morning and afternoon, I need to stay available into my local evening. With flex time I can usually then work for a shorter period some other day that week (usually a Friday). But it's still not unusual for me to work 10-12 hour days, or longer. My family and I have to be willing to accept that to make this arrangement work.

As you can see, working in a different time zone requires a fair amount of flexibility in the hours you are willing to work. But it's worth noting that you can make the shift work to your advantage. When I'm facing a deadline, for example, those four to five hours in the morning without distracting calls, e-mails, messages, etc. are invaluable. As noted in the last chapter, you may not want to put this forward as a reason to work remotely, as you don't want to give the impression that you are less productive now than you could be. But once you are established in place, you will want to take full advantage of any time shift to maximize your productivity.

Staying In Touch

The specifics for how you will communicate with your customers and colleagues depend on your company's network infrastructure as well as your personal style. But once you are off-site, it doesn't matter how far off-site, so long as you have a reliable internet connection.

There are both hardware and software solutions for maintaining connectivity. One approach is to use a Virtual Private Network (VPN) router to securely connect your laptop and a Voice over Internet Protocol (VoIP) phone to your company's network. This provides constant network access and allows people to reach you via a U.S. phone

extension to a physical phone. Another approach is to connect via a home router using VPN software. Software such
as Skype Enterprise Voice can handle U.S. and international phone communications, which can be accessed through a
laptop and headset. Having the flexibility to make and take
calls anywhere in the world via a laptop may be attractive
for many workers. It will also allow you to take calls as
normal when you make a site visit, as opposed to having to
transfer your extension as you would with a physical
phone. If you do end up primarily communicating through
your laptop, make sure you procure a quality headset as
you'll likely be wearing it for several hours each day.

Mobile phones are another consideration. If your company has issued you a U.S. cell phone, it may be impracti-
cal to take it abroad due to network incompatibilities and
roaming expenses. But you might not need it anyway since
you will be working from home and will almost always be
in one primary location. And if your setup supports it, you
may be able to make and receive calls through your laptop
when you are not in your home office.

A cell phone may be helpful for communicating via
SMS text messages, as people are often on the go. If this is
important to you, after you move you can get an international cell phone that lets you make and receive text messages via Wi-Fi. Or use Google+ Hangouts or apps like
Facebook Messenger or WhatsApp. In my case, I returned
my company-issued cell phone when I moved and purchased a personal phone from a German company instead.
It's an unlocked phone, so I purchased a sim card that gives

me a U.S. phone number that I use during my site visits. I've found T-Mobile's Prepaid and Pay As You Go plans well-suited for my occasional need for a U.S. phone and data plan.

The telecommunications equipment provided to teleworkers will probably be part of your teleworker agreement. But you will still want to contact your company's information technology department to determine the best communications setup for your situation. (You can also see the Resources section of my website for links to articles about technologies that help you stay in touch.)

Staying Engaged

Any teleworking arrangement means you have to put in some extra effort to execute collaborative tasks and maintain your working identity. The random drop-ins... the side discussions as you file out of meetings... the serendipitous comments you overhear in the hallway or at the copier... sometimes these are distractions, but often they yield valuable insights and connections. There's also the space you occupy in other people's heads by having your face visible around the office. You lose all this when you telework and so you will need to put in extra effort to stay engaged with your customers and colleagues.

These issues are generally the same whether you are working stateside or internationally, with the main difference being to the great challenge or impossibility of being in the office on short notice. In my case, I spend much time in technical calls and meetings with my colleagues throughout the working day and so I am able to stay well-engaged. But I have still found the following strategies critical for staying disciplined and engaged with the office:

- One-on-one tag-ups with key people, at least weekly. You need to connect with people as much as possible to pick up on the little insights and connections you will miss from being out of the office.
- Make extra effort to talk during meetings and to follow-up afterwards. If you are on the phone for a meeting and most people are in the room, it can be easy to just let them do the talking for you. But this comes with the risk of people forgetting what you do and how you contribute. Don't talk for the sake of people hearing your voice, but don't hesitate to jump in the conversation when you have something to say, either. Also, if there are people in the meeting that you don't interact with as often, make an extra effort to call them afterwards to continue any discussions that were left unresolved.
- Return to the office periodically. Even with regular calls, people still need to see your face to remember that they can still count on you as a resource.
- Use instant messenger applications heavily. These are very helpful for you to maintain a real-time presence even while overseas.
- Depending on your company's culture and your personal style, you might consider video teleconferencing. I'll just note that I personally have never

found it necessary. Voice communications have been fully sufficient.

- Have a support network in the office to help you with matters requiring an in-person interaction. If a critical presentation needs to be given face-to-face and it is impossible for you to return in time, is there someone who can deliver it on your behalf? If there is an occasional site-specific, laboratory component to your work, can you delegate it during the times when you can't be there?

Consider also work and relationship development over the longer term. You may be secure in your current network and job duties, and so it's an easy transition to remote work. However, change is constant, as we all know. While you maintain your existing relationships, focus also on developing new ones that may lead to generating new work and projects. Because this challenge increases significantly when you aren't there in person, you need to leverage your site visits for face-to-face relationship development and maintenance as much as possible.

Site Visits

It is unlikely that you can make a long-term international telework arrangement succeed without returning periodically to your main work site. Of course how often you return will depend on your personal situation. As I mentioned earlier, I typically travel back three to four times per year in order to recharge my collaborative work and remain in people's "headspace." It's easy to start feeling disconnected and isolated over time when working remotely, and site visits are a good way to rekindle your own personal motivation. Finally, as noted in the previous section, your work environment can change quickly. Site visits can be a key tool for establishing new relationships that lead to new work opportunities. This helps maintain the stability of your agreement and reduces the risk that you'll be asked to return to the United States before you are ready.

Due to the cost and time involved with international travel, try to plan your trips deliberately and establish an objective beforehand for each one. Besides the general goal of reconnecting with your team, your management, and your customers, think about any important meetings coming up that would be to your benefit to attend in person, and plan your trip around those. If you have some control over scheduling, you could plan to have these key meetings while you are there. If your department or division is planning a team-building exercise, especially one that is off-site, you'll probably want to attend if you can. And finally, be sure to schedule one-on-one tag-ups with as many people as possible – especially your boss. This way you will get more candid insights than you might otherwise in a general meeting or over the phone.

To be a successful teleworker, you want the people you work with to trust that you are very much still part of the team. As bonding with your colleagues can sometimes be more effective during non-work functions, consider scheduling some of your trips back around major work-related social functions such as department lunches, off-site social events, retirement parties, etc. In addition, you might be proactive about getting together socially with your colleagues after work, for example during a happy hour. If you go out of your way to be social with your team during your visits back, you will probably find yourself feeling more engaged than if you only socialized at the office during work hours.

Depending on what you negotiated in your teleworking agreement, you may be looking at picking up some or all of your travel expenses. Here are some strategies that may help you minimize your or your company's travel costs:

Flights

Depending on where you move to, air travel will probably be your most significant expense. If you are responsible for paying for your own flights, you will want to consider a variety of strategies to lower your costs. First, if your home and/or work site are close to any major airline hubs, you will likely find cheaper ticket prices with the dominant carrier. If you haven't already, be sure to sign up for that airline's frequent flier program. If they have a credit card program, that may be another way to accumulate mileage.

Ticket prices are most expensive during peak seasons (summer and winter breaks) and cheaper during off-peak times. But the mileage amounts required for a given trip are usually the same (though there may be fewer mileage tickets available during peak season). If you will be flying back during both peak (say, summer) and off-peak (say, February or March) times, consider buying your tickets for the off-peak trips and then using your miles for trips during peak season.

In addition to using your miles effectively, be sure to price shop with other airlines even if they aren't dominant at your hub. Often you will find the best prices with the main carrier, but not always. For example, I live close to Frankfurt and I often fly to Washington DC. Normally I get the best fares with Lufthansa and United; however, Iceland Air also offers service between these cities with a plane change in Reykjavik. Sometimes the difference in cost is several hundred dollars, but other times it is much less than that. When the cost difference is minor, I am usually willing to pay a little bit more to fly non-stop on the majors and collect the miles.

Rental Car

If you need a rental car when you are back stateside, it's easy to find a good price using travel sites such as Kayak, Expedia, Orbitz, etc. But as you choose your rental agency provider, make sure they have a frequent flier arrangement with your preferred carrier to help you accumulate miles faster and reduce your flight costs.

When renting a car, you will want to pay special attention to the various kinds of insurance you will need. Your foreign automobile insurance may not cover damage, loss, and liability while driving a rental car in the United States, so be sure you understand your policy. You could also look at using a credit card with *primary* rental car insurance benefits versus secondary benefits. With a primary benefit, the card issuer assumes the cost before other insurance kicks in. With a secondary benefit, the card only assumes costs after the primary insurance is exhausted. If you do not have a primary insurance (such as personal auto insurance), your secondary policy through your card may or may not become the primary for any damage or loss. So, be sure you fully understand your card's benefits and terms.

It is not difficult to find a credit card with primary or secondary benefits that cover you for damage or loss of the rental car. However, very few cards protect against injury, personal liability, and damage to other vehicles and personal property. If your foreign primary policy does not offer those benefits, you will need to find a way to purchase the proper insurance. The easiest, but probably most expensive option is through the rental agency when you reserve or pick up your vehicle. But you might also try contacting auto insurance companies for a short-term policy. GEICO, for example, offers a six-month policy that provides all necessary coverage while you are in the United States. If you are going to be at your site for a couple weeks or more, you may find that a policy through a major provider costs the same, or even less, than going through the rental car agency.

One additional consideration: many companies have negotiated rates with rental car agencies that include all of the necessary insurance for when you travel on business. If you compare what it would cost to rent a car on your own with the rental agency's insurance, it may be cheaper for you to rent through your company's travel system – even if the daily rate is a little higher. So in your negotiation, ask your company to cover the rental car expense while you are in town, or at least let you use its travel system to reserve it. In sum, before you purchase a rental car agency's often pricey insurance, be sure you understand the terms and costs of your other options.

Lodging

As with rental cars, most major hotel chains have loyalty programs that provide points or rewards to reduce the cost of future stays. In many cases these points can be applied to frequent flier programs. So if your goal is to minimize your flight cost by accumulating miles quickly, find a hotel chain with a loyalty program that can help you do that.

If paying for a hotel is more expense than you would like, consider what's available through Airbnb or an equivalent. But before you do that, consider if you really need to stay somewhere commercial in the first place. Do you have family or friends with a guest bedroom that would be willing to let you stay with them when you visit? Lodging can end up being a significant expense and asking to stay with others is the best way to avoid it. Plus, it's a great opportunity to catch up with them. If you will be making a couple trips a year, you can try to spread out your requests so that you are only staying at one place per year. And to reciprocate the generosity of those you stay with, be sure to offer to host and lodge them if they plan a vacation to see your exciting new country!

Travel Time

When traveling to your site, clarify with your company whether you are doing that on your own time or theirs. Since you are the one asking to telework, your management may not be open to your travel being on company time. However, if you have flex time and are concerned about the travel, you could work during the flight and then charge those hours as if you were at home.

Checking In With Your Boss

A regularly scheduled tag-up with your boss may or may not be necessary, depending on your situation. But again, your prime strategy for success is to make sure you are available when needed, especially with your management. It is important to proactively check in with your boss from time to time about how she thinks it is going. When at your work site in person, this would be an excellent time to meet with your boss, and perhaps even your boss's boss, to see if they are developing any concerns about your arrangement. If she starts to become worried about your absence or level of engagement, you can discuss ways to mitigate those concerns before it gets to the point where she wants you to return. Conversely, if you achieve transparency and she is happy with your engagement and performance, she will remain your ally in assuaging any engagement concerns coming from further up the management chain.

Other Resources

There are plenty of other strategies that you can employ to stay engaged while working remotely. You will find your way through a good initial plan and then paying attention to what works. Probably your best sources of information will be talking to other successful teleworkers in your company about their work habits and lessons learned. But for more, you can also go to the Resources section of my website that includes links to additional successful teleworking strategies.

CHAPTER 6

Making the Move

Start by doing what is necessary, then what is possible, and suddenly you are doing the impossible.

— Francis of Assisi

This chapter summarizes some of the other practicalities when moving outside of the United States. Again, I am not an attorney or tax expert, so take this as general information only. You will want to consult professionals as you navigate the areas described in this chapter, especially since the specifics of your situation depend on factors such as where you want to move, personal goals, company policies, etc. However, this chapter should get you started on whom you need to talk to and what questions to ask.

Moving Abroad

The logistics involved in moving abroad are intimidating. But the degree of difficulty depends on whether you only plan to be away for a short time and maintain property in the United States, versus a full relocation. My wife and I did the latter; we sold our house in the U.S., bought a new one in Germany, moved over what possessions we could, and sold the rest. So I've probably been through one of the more difficult cases of moving abroad and can speak from experience that it's not as daunting as it first seems.

Finding a place to live in your new country may be challenging as you can only afford to make one or two exploratory trips. So it's important to perform extensive research ahead of time, identify your search criteria, and then focus on visiting the best housing candidates when you visit in person. Before you arrive, you can look online for realtors in the areas that interest you. They can help you narrow down your search and prioritize which properties to view. Joining an online expat group can also help in your search. You can, for example, ask the group for their take on the desirability of locations under consideration. You might even ask someone to send you unbiased photos of a property you are interested in as a way to help you put together your list of candidates.

A full review of the logistics of moving abroad is beyond the scope of this book. However, you may be surprised in the end to discover how similar it is to a domestic move. Many moving companies operate internationally and can walk you through the process. Usually this involves deciding on the volume you want to have transported and selecting the appropriate-sized shipping container. On moving day the container is driven to your residence on a flatbed truck, packed just like a normal moving van, sealed, put on a ship, put through local customs, and then delivered to your new residence. If you don't completely fill a container, the moving company may help you share it with another customer and offset some of the cost.

Moving costs and transport time will vary significantly by country. Therefore you may want to factor these into your country selection process. If so, feel free to contact any of the major moving companies to ask if they can provide you cost and time estimates for your countries of interest.

Finally, if you have a lot of possessions and have been looking to downsize and declutter, moving abroad may be a great opportunity to do so. You can decide that you don't want to take any more than what fits in a particular container space and sell the rest, perhaps via an estate sale. There are many companies that will help you with this undertaking. My family of five fit everything we needed into a 20 foot container, and it was quite liberating to dispose of all that household clutter and cheap furniture that we'd been carrying around for years. If you don't want to sell your excess belongings, there is always the option of asking family and friends to store them, or renting a long-term storage unit.

Taxes

Taxes may be the most complicated issue you will have to figure out when living abroad. Again, I am neither an accountant nor tax attorney, so take what I say as general information based on my own personal experience. You will obviously need to determine your own situation in consultation with tax professionals. Also, tax policies and treaties are subject to change, so my personal experiences here may no longer be relevant by the time you read this. With these caveats in mind, here is what I've found with respect to filing U.S. taxes while living abroad:

Federal Taxes

As the United States still maintains citizen-based taxation (vs. residence-based), you will have to continue to file a U.S. Federal Tax return for as long as you are a citizen, even if you do not reside in the United States. The good news is that you can probably use the Foreign Earned Income Exclusion to eliminate your U.S. tax liability below a certain threshold to avoid some double taxation. (In 2018, the threshold amount is $104,100.) In addition, you may be able to claim the Foreign Tax Credit to reduce your U.S. taxes based on income taxes you pay to a foreign government. These provisions do not appear to have been affected by the Tax Cuts and Job Act passed on January 1, 2018. As of this writing the full implications of the new law are still emerging and you should consult your tax advisor to be sure you understand how it will impact your situation.

You will also need to consider whether you will have U.S. or your host country's income taxes withheld from your paycheck. This depends on your company's tax compliance policies, your host country's tax treaty with the United States (if it has one), and how long you plan to stay abroad. Note that if you borrow money to buy property in a foreign country, your foreign mortgage interest may still be deductible from your U.S. return, up to the new limit of $750,000.

If you establish full residency in a foreign country, but continue to have U.S. Federal Taxes withheld as normal, you may need to make quarterly income tax pre-payments directly to your local tax office. Then, if the timing works out, you can file your U.S. return before your local return is due and apply the balance of your refund to any additional local taxes owed. You will need to consult with your local tax authority to ensure that you are pre-paying enough to avoid triggering penalties for underpayment.

State Taxes

If you are only moving abroad for a temporary term and are leaving a state or territory that collects its own taxes, and you intend to keep your property and other ties there, you will likely need to continue to pay your state, local, and property tax obligations (though your resident/non-resident status may change). If you are moving abroad for longer, and don't specifically plan to return to your former state, you may no longer be required to pay state taxes as long as you completely sever your residency. But be careful here!

This could be a dangerous trap as there are horror stories of expats who stopped state withholding while living abroad, but failed to sufficiently sever their ties. Then, after a couple years, they were hit with major tax bills and penalties from their former state of residence for unpaid income taxes. California, South Carolina, Virginia, and New Mexico are apparently the more difficult states to sever residency from. So if you intend to sever your state residency and stop paying state taxes, you will need to take appropriate steps.

In my case, I moved from Virginia, one of the more difficult states, so I was careful to fully establish my residency in Germany, and sever my state and local ties. This included selling my Virginia property, allowing my driver's license to expire, closing all local bank accounts, etc. I then filed my last state tax return for the year I moved as a part-year resident. This seems to have been sufficient. If you intend to sever your ties and stop your state tax withholding, be sure you understand your state tax residency requirements and are prepared to take all the necessary steps to avoid being hit with future penalties.

Tax Services

There are numerous tax preparation services available to help expats with their U.S. taxes. I use one and they are invaluable for demystifying my tax obligations and answering questions throughout the year. I also use a separate tax preparer in my local host country. There are international tax firms that can handle both sides, but I've found them to be extremely expensive. It my case it is sufficient, and far cheaper, to work with both an expat preparer and a local preparer. I've included some links to expat tax preparation services on my website, thought this does not constitute an endorsement of any particular organization.

Once again – the tax implications of moving abroad will probably be the most complicated issue you and your company will face. The information in this section hopefully gives you an idea for the questions you need to start asking. You can start your tax research via the links on my website, but you will obviously want to consult with your company's tax and legal departments as well as your own accountant.

Your Paycheck and Foreign Bank Accounts

Depending on your company, you might be paid in your local currency or you might be paid in dollars. The advantage to getting paid in the local currency is that you avoid arbitrage and transfer fees, but your company may not be willing or able to go through the hassle and expense of assuming that responsibility. If not, you can maintain a bank account in the United States, have your pay deposited directly, and then transfer it as needed to your account at your local bank. Numerous services exist to do this, some more expensive than others. If you continue to be paid in dollars, a fluctuating exchange rate can have significant positive or negative consequences to your overall effective salary. So don't forget to factor the exchange rate, purchasing power, and transfer fees into your overall financial plan.

Be aware that foreign assets and money you have in a foreign bank account that exceed a certain threshold need to be declared to the IRS via a report of Foreign Bank and Financial Accounts (FBAR) filing or FATCA Form 8938. This is not difficult to do and many expat tax services can help you with it. There can be major penalties for failing to declare your foreign assets and accounts, so be sure you file either or both of these if required!

Certificate of Coverage

As described in Social Security in Chapter 3, there will likely be social security tax implications for your living abroad. To avoid having to pay into each country's system against the same earnings, you will want to apply for a Certificate of Coverage (COC) via the Social Security Administration to prove to your host country that you are paying into the U.S. system. For most countries, an initial COC is only valid for up to five years, though extensions are possible. It is recommended, though not required, that you apply for and receive your COC before you move abroad.

If you plan to stay in your selected country for a period shorter than the five years typically allowed under a COC, then you will likely want to continue to pay into the U.S. Social Security system as normal. If you plan to live in your host country past your COC duration, you will have to change to start paying into its system, unless you are able to get an extension. If you do end up switching from the U.S. Social Security system to that of your host country, the Totalization agreements allow for the benefits from the United States and your host country to be combined if you've paid into both systems for a sufficient amount of time. (You can find out more about this in the country-by-country Totalization Agreement details on the Social Security Administration website, which I've linked to in the Resources section of this book and on my website.)

Voting

Moving to a foreign country does not mean you have to give up your right to vote. You will need to register as an expat voter in the state you last had residence in so you can continue to vote at least in national elections. After I did this, I still receive absentee ballots for state and local elections, but I've not found a satisfactory opinion about whether this is factored into state residency severability (see the earlier State Taxes discussion). So to be safe, I continue to vote in national elections, though not in local ones. You will need to assess this risk for yourself if you intend to sever your state residency.

Health Insurance

Multinational companies will usually have an international health insurance option that you can select. With this, you may have to pay for your foreign medical services directly, then file a claim. If your company does not offer this, you will need to find out what your current medical insurance covers while you are abroad, or you can investigate your country of interest's public or private health insurance options.

Estate Planning

If the worst happens while you are living abroad, what will happen to your assets and which country's laws will apply? You will want to consult estate planning attorneys in both countries to draft the appropriate documents that avoid forcing your family to untangle what could be a very messy situation. Since state laws typically govern estate planning considerations, this becomes especially important if you've severed your state residency.

Investments

Investment firms have extra reporting requirements for clients that do not reside in the United States. To avoid this, some firms only will accept American clients, or at least .clients with U.S. addresses. You will therefore want to investigate the potential of being forced to transfer or sell your investment assets if you can no longer provide your broker with a U.S. mailing address.

More Help

The totality of you need to do to establish yourself in a foreign country depends on your personal situation, the country you select, and how long you want to stay there. Specific details vary by country and are thus beyond the scope of this book. However, it's easy to find help.

Social media is an amazing tool for anyone looking to move abroad. Facebook, for example, has expat groups for seemingly every country in the world. Here, Americans and locals can interact and ask each other questions on almost any imaginable topic. For example, I've seen people join German Facebook expat groups months before their move to get an idea of what to expect, ask for tips on navigating the local bureaucracies, and learn how to fit in and avoid problems once they arrive. If you don't want to sign up for a social media site, you can search for other country-specific, expat-supporting websites and discussion boards. There are also companies that specialize in helping expats meet people and integrate into the local culture. You can find them with a simple web search.

And of course you can always go to my website, www.teleworkabroad.com, to find articles on more specialized topics and additional, up-to-date links to further resources.

CHAPTER 7

Making It Last

A mind that is stretched by a new experience can never go back to its old dimensions.

— Oliver Wendell Holmes

Now that you are established and everything is in place, it's time to start taking the longer view. When as you contemplate your future, you may start asking:

1. *How long __can__ I stay?*

2. *How long do I __want__ to stay?*

As you become established in your new country and learn more about the international rules and regulations covering your arrangement, the amount of time you can stay abroad may ends up being less than the amount of time you would wish to stay. Therefore it is important to gain an awareness of any practical limits that may force you to return before you are ready, and then contrast that with your personal goals for being abroad.

Your Practical Limit

There will likely be a practical limit for how long you can telework internationally. This limit has to do with if your company has a limited teleworking policy, whether you can outstay your Social Security Certificate of Coverage, and whether you have a limited residency permit or visa from your host country. There are likely ways to extend your stay around these limits, but they depend on the specifics of your particular situation.

Your ability to remain effective in your job, and your management's willingness to manage the hassle of you being remote, are also major factors in how long you are able to stay – but are more under your control. As described in Chapter 5, your paramount goal is for your teleworking to remain as transparent as possible to your management and colleagues. When your boss can't really tell the difference between your situation and that of others who are working from home or one state over, you know you are approaching success. Do everything you can to stay engaged, check in with your boss about how it's going from her perspective, and she will become your ally in helping to manage any concerns coming from further up the chain that may limit your time abroad.

Your Personal Limit

You also have a personal limit, which has to do with your family and career goals, your integration into your new society, and whether you are getting what you want out of the experience.

To be honest, integrating into a foreign society or culture can be extremely rewarding, but it also hard. There are challenges, frustrations, regrets "...*had I only known!*" This is compounded if you are learning the local language on top of figuring out again how everything around you works. Rest assured this is all normal and you will find your way. Procedures and customs that are strange and frustrating today will soon become natural in the not-too-distant future. If you are hit with major culture shock in your first few weeks – give it some time. I'd say plan on staying at least two to three years to start hitting your stride and feeling like you are at home.

So what if you and your family end up enjoying your lives in your new host country and you decide you want to stay for the long term? In the best case, your practical and personal limits will not be in conflict and you will be able to stay as long as you wish. When you are ready to move back to the United States, you can do it on your own terms and at a time of your choosing. But what if your personal limit exceeds your practical limit?

If you find yourself not really wanting to move back to the United States, think about the maximum duration your company will likely support you being abroad. You will already have an idea of this from the proposal and negotiation process, but you should still realistically assess: "Will my company really allow me to do this for X more years? Maybe even until retirement? And do I really want to work remotely for that long? If I want to stay longer than what my company will likely allow, how hard will it be for me to find a local job?"

If you want to stay in your country but don't realistically expect to be able to retire from your company as an international teleworker, you need to develop your strategy for how to stay past your job. Some of your options include:

- If your company has an active operation in the country you are in, you might apply for a transfer to one of those sites (after considering the pros and cons discussed in Chapter 2).

- You can resign and work with a PEO to contract back out to your company, or become a self-employed consultant (as discussed in Chapter 3).

- You can resign and then find a job with a local company, assuming you have achieved permanent resident status and/or have obtained a valid work permit.

- You can find a job with another American company that has operations in your chosen country.

- You can go into business for yourself, maybe even developing additional income streams while you telework with your main job. This way, if you ever face the choice of resigning or returning sooner than you'd like, you will still have an income source that can support you during a transition period.

Hopefully you have put into place an agreement that works well for both you and your company and it is sustainable for as long as you want it to be. But don't be surprised if you thrive while living abroad and want to stay longer than what your company may allow. You would be wise to prepare yourself for this possibility.

CHAPTER 8

In a Nutshell

Chance favors the prepared mind.

— Louis Pasteur

The following list sums up the key things you need to do along the way of becoming an international teleworker. It can be used as a quick reference checklist as you research and plan your strategy. You can refer to previous chapters for detailed discussions of each item.

1. **Understand the advantages and challenges of becoming an international teleworker.**

   - Where do you want to live and why? What do you expect will be better or worse than where you live now?

   - Determine how compatible this will be with your life and career goals. Will this help or slow down your career? Will your family be willing to make sacrifices alongside you?

   - Determine if full-time telework in general appeals to you. Talk to other remote workers and consider a trial run of working from home if you aren't sure.

2. **Consider your value to your company and how suited your current work is to being done remotely.**

   - Start making any needed changes.

   - Reinforce your relationships with your management chain.

   - Seek out experience leading or being part of a virtual team.

3. **Research your company's current teleworker policies and procedures.**

   - Determine how compatible they are with your goals.

   - Talk to other full-time teleworkers in your company about their lessons learned.

4. **Find out whether your company already has operations in your country of interest.**

- Would it be a good fit for you to transfer to one of those groups?

- Will this reduce your company's foreign income tax risk and reporting and compliance costs?

- If the risk of setting up a Permanent Establishment is likely to be a problem, consider whether an International PEO or self-employed consultant role are potential alternate paths for you.

5. **Determine what living in your country of interest will mean for you in terms of:**

- Desired lifestyle, for you and your spouse.

- Your children's education and future prospects.

- U.S. Federal and State income taxes.

- Your host country's income taxes.

- Social Security taxes.

- Health insurance.

- Investments and estate planning.

- Moving costs.

6. **Make your final country selection. Ensure that it offers:**

- A stable and reliable residential internet connection

- Reasonable access to major transportation hubs to facilitate visits back to your work site.

7. **Research a positive business case for your company.**

   - Why should your management let you do this? (Is it justification enough that they will keep you on as an employee?)
   - Will your company save money moving you off site?
   - Can your company leverage your presence abroad for recruiting or business development?

8. **Determine what you are willing to accept with respect to:**

   - Your departure date.
   - How long you can stay.
   - Your core work hours and flexibility.
   - Frequency of site visits.
   - Sharing of site visit travel costs.
   - Help with international tax and miscellaneous logistics expenses.

9. **Develop your initial strategies for:**

   - Managing any time shift.
   - Technologies to use to stay in touch.
   - Staying engaged with your team and your management.
   - Minimizing the travel costs of site visits.

10. **Present your proposal.**

11. **Listen to your management's concerns and negotiate and adapt as needed.**

12. **Document your international telework agreement.**

13. **Make the move.**
    - Reach out to others already living in your country of interest for advice on integration and where to live.
    - Apply for your COC.
    - Adjust your tax withholding as needed.
    - Sever your state residency if desired.

14. **Employ effective telework strategies to ensure you return on your terms.**
    - Stay engaged and prove your productivity.
    - Build new relationships / develop new work.
    - Have regular tag ups with colleagues and check-ins with your management.
    - Make regular site visits.

15. **Have a strategy for what to do if you decide you want to stay longer than what your company (or country) will normally allow.**

Postscript

Twenty years from now you will be more disappointed by the things you didn't do than by the ones you did do.

— Mark Twain

First, thank you for reading this book! As I said up front, I love living abroad and I love my U.S.-based job. I was fortunate to find a way to have both and I want to help you if this is your goal as well. If you are still in the dreaming stage, I hope this has inspired you to action and to start putting your plan in place to make it happen. With a bit of forethought, research, negotiation, and best practices, you can make it work as well.

If you are planning to telework internationally, or already are, I would love to hear from you! Please send me an e-mail at penhallegon@teleworkabroad.com to tell me your story and make any suggestions for improving future versions of this book. I'm also happy to answer any further questions you might have that weren't already covered in these pages. Please also visit my website at www.teleworkabroad.com for more resources, articles, and tips. If you found this book helpful, I would greatly appreciate if you could leave a review on Amazon.

Thank you again for reading. It's a big world – now get out in it!

Online Resources

The more that you read, the more things you will know. The more that you learn, the more places you'll go.

– Dr. Seuss

The links below include more detail on many of the topics addressed in this book.

Telework Abroad
- Stop by my website to find articles on more specialized topics and additional links to resources mentioned in this book.
- http://www.teleworkabroad.com

Teleworking Statistics
- Global Workplace Analytics offers a wealth of information about teleworking trends and benefits to individuals and employers. Their website is well worth reviewing as you develop your proposal. They also provide calculators to help you figure out how much you and employer might save.
- http://globalworkplaceanalytics.com/telecommuting-statistics

TelCoa: The Telework Coalition
- TelCoa is a telework advocacy group that promotes the awareness and acceptance of the benefits of working remotely. Many of the multi-state telework advantages they discuss also apply to the international case, and are worth reviewing as you develop your proposal.
- https://www.telcoa.org/

"Checklist for international telecommuting"
- This is a helpful list of things employers will need to consider when allowing international telework. You should be familiar with these as you develop your proposal.
- https://www.accountingweb.com/practice/team/checklist-for-international-telecommuting

Social Security Totalization Agreements and Certificates of Coverage
- The Social Security Administration describes the Totalization Agreements with each country and allows you to apply for a COC for when you are abroad.
- Totalization Agreement Descriptions: https://www.ssa.gov/international/agreement_descriptions.html
- Apply for a COC: https://www.ssa.gov/international/CoC_link.html

Acknowledgements

I would like to thank my company, my management, and my direct supervisor for allowing me to follow my dream of living abroad. Though I have tried to minimize the administrative burden on them wherever possible, I recognize that it can't be fully eliminated and I deeply appreciate their willingness to help me make this happen.

I would like to thank my brother, Douglas Penhallegon, for a thorough and exemplary edit of this manuscript. Any mistakes in language or grammar remain because I did not follow his advice. Thanks also to my colleague and fellow international teleworker, Amber Sprenger, for reading and providing thoughtful suggestions and additions. And finally, I would like to thank my wonderful wife Sybille for encouraging me to live abroad and for figuring out many of the practical details that I cover in these pages.

ABOUT THE AUTHOR

William Penhallegon lives with his family near
Heidelberg, Germany and works as a manager and
engineer for a not-for-profit company based in the
Washington D.C. area. He writes about international
telework at www.teleworkabroad.com.